D1253838

AT THE TURNING

AT THE
TURNING

Three Addresses on Judaism

By MARTIN BUBER

FARRAR, STRAUS AND YOUNG

New York

TABLE OF CONTENTS

These three addresses have been delivered in November and December 1951 in New York, as the Israel Goldstein Lectures for that year, under the auspices of the Jewish Theological Seminary.

The reader should bear in mind, that a Jew speaks here to Jews, in the center of the Diaspora, in the hour when the deciding crisis of Judaism begins to become manifest.

JUDAISM AND CIVILIZATION

Judaism and Civilization

To RECOGNIZE the nature of what we call a "great
civilization," we must consider the great historical
civilizations not at the time of their full development but at an early stage. We shall then see that
each of them can be understood only as a life-system.
In distinction to a thought-system, which illuminates
and elucidates the spheres of being from a central
idea, a life-system is the real unit in which again and
again the spheres of existence of a historical group build
up around a supreme principle. This principle achieves
adequate consciousness and articulateness only in
sublime moments of the spirit, but its effect pervades,
in manifold ramifications and shapes, and, of course,
also in varying degrees of intensity, the entire existence of the group. Its fundamental character is always
a religious and normative one: a religious one, because
it always implies an attachment of human life to the

absolute, an attachment which, though susceptible of intellectual comprehension, is essentially concrete, means concrete things, and points to concrete
things; and a normative one, because the principle,
though always relating to transcendent Being controlling the universe, proclaims that Being as exemplary
for man, as that which alone, if imitated by man in his
life-attitude and social structure, brings order and
meaning into earthly existence, and on whose realization on earth by man depends, in fact, the survival
of man qua man.

Whether we take the Chinese principle of *tao*,
the "way" in whose eternal rhythm all opposites contend with each other and are reconciled, or the Indo-
Aryan *rita* (Indian form) or *urta* (Iranian form, usually transcribed *asha*), the primeval order of that
which is right and just, or Israel's *tsedek*, in which
truth and justice combine, or the Greek *dike*, the
inexorable course of world events, and the "measure"
determined by it — everywhere transcendent Being
has a side facing toward man which represents a
shall-be; everywhere man, if he wants to exist as man,
must strive after a super-human model; everywhere,
the outline of a true human society is traced in
Heaven. All spheres of existence are essentially determined by that principle, by the relationship to
it; wisdom wants to explore its action, art to lend

shape to it, and where one strives to set public life itself to rights, one looks up to the stars and beyond them.

Man as he is (who in all these doctrines appears more or less as out of joint, having lost his original concord with transcendent Being) naturally resists the command which he, man, has either read from the universe or received directly from a power superior to him and to the universe. He wills and wills not to translate the heavenly truth into earthly reality. He rebels in practice against what he recognizes in theory, nay, what he sees and hears. But it is precisely in this mute struggle of man with the spirit that the rise of a great civilization originates. The spirit conquers and is conquered, it advances and is checked, it hits upon the human materia and finds in it a barrier; and here, in the lulls of the fighting between Heaven and earth, there emerge, again and again, the specific forms of a civilization which also determine all its wisdom and art.

Among the great civilizations of the ancient world there was one in which the action of the religious and normative principle upon all spheres of public life manifested itself with peculiar, unique pregnancy. All others shared, though in varying degrees of development, the basic doctrine of a heavenly-cosmic society to which the earthly, human one corresponds or rather ought to correspond — to which it corresponded once, say in the Golden Age, or will correspond some day, say after the complete victory of light over darkness. In ancient Israel, the place of this doctrine was taken by that of the Lord of all being and all coming to be, Who, just as He has set the sun in the sky, has set the commandment of truth and justice above the heads of the human race. True, in the other civilizations as well, the normative principle was carried and guaranteed by divine beings who ruled that upper society; but only Israel knew a God Who had chosen a human people — just that people — to prepare the created earth as a kingdom for Him by the realization of justice. For Israel, the principle is the norm and the law, for Israel's God it is the mobile foundation, symbolized by the Ark with the Tables, on which He wants to place His earthly throne. This is why the principle here binds the deity and mankind together in the unparalleled concreteness of the "Covenant." And this is also why here, and only here, civilization is mysteriously both affirmed and negated: God wants man's entire civilization — but not as left to itself but as hallowed to Him, God.

Now we generally observe that man's resistance to the spiritual demand, a resistance which, as we said, manifests itself already in the genetic phase of a civilization, increases decisively as the civilization

approaches its height. In proportion to the development of its specific forms, every civilization strives
increasingly to render itself independent of its principle. In the great Western civilizations, this manifests
itself partly by their individual spheres isolating themselves and each of them establishing its own basis and
order, and partly by the principle itself losing its
absolute character and validity, so that the holy norm
degenerates into a human convention, or by the
attachment to the absolute being reduced, avowedly
or unavowedly, to a mere symbolic-ritual requirement,
which may be adequately satisfied in the cultic
sphere. A civilization may now, in its isolated individual spheres, produce works more splendid than
it has ever produced before; its spiritual unity is lost.
Periclean Athens and the Italian High Renaissance
may serve as examples. The development of the
Eastern civilizations was different. Here, the individual spheres never fully emancipated themselves
from the unifying bond, but even here the principle
became more and more an object of doctrine rather
than of life-relationship, and its service, originally
embracing real existence, both private and historical,
became more and more a merely symbolic and formal
one. And here as well as there, the civilization, by
converting the principle by whose action it had first
arisen from an active reality into a revered fiction,

undermined its own foundations.

Everywhere there were men who recognized this movement towards the abyss for what it was and tried to halt it; but there was only one civilization in which an elemental protest, concentrating all the spiritual passion of the people, was raised against the invalidation of the principle. It was, naturally enough, that civilization in which, as in no other, the absolute had made a covenant with the entire domain of human existence and refused to abandon any part of that domain to relativity. At no other time or place has the spirit been served in the human world with such militancy, generation after generation, as it was by the prophets of Israel. Here, the men of spirit took it upon themselves to actualize that affirmation and negation of civilization in the reality of the historical hour. Their fight was directed against all those who evaded the great duty, the duty of actualizing the divine truth in the fullness of everyday life, by side-stepping into the merely formal, the merely ritual, that is to say, the noncommittal — all those who taught and practiced such evasion and thereby degraded the divine name which they invoked to the status of a carefully guarded fiction. This fight was waged for the wholeness and unity of civilization, which can be whole and united only if it is hallowed to God. The men who demanded from those in power the abolition of social injustice for God's sake did not know the concept of civilization, but they staked their lives to save civilization. Thereby, the protest against the false emancipation of civilization was registered in such a way that it was bound to act, and did in fact act, as a reminder and warning, upon the whole future of mankind, and quite especially upon the problematics of the last following civilization, that of the Christian West.

To appreciate fully the significance of prophetic religion for mankind and its civilization, we must ask ourselves why it was precisely in Israel that the normative principle voiced its protest against any such development of civilization as tended to deprive it, the normative principle, of its absolute validity. In answer, we must point to that religious realism peculiar to Israel which has no room for a truth remaining abstract, hovering self-sufficiently above reality, but for which every truth is bound up with a demand which man, the people, Israel are called upon to fulfill integrally on earth. Now integral fulfillment means two things: it must, in the first place, comprise the whole life, the whole civilization of a people, economy, society, and state, and secondly, it must incorporate the whole of the individual, his emotions and his will, his actions and abstentions, his life at home and in the market place, in the temple and in the popular assembly. That is to say, it means the wholeness and unity — not otherwise possible — of the civilization. Men, especially the possessors of power and property, naturally resist the demand for the integral fulfillment of divine truth and justice; they, therefore, try to limit the service of God to the sacral sphere, and in all other spheres recognize his authority merely by words and symbols. This is where the prophetic protest sets in.

A characteristic example may illustrate our point. In the ancient East, the king was generally regarded as a son of the supreme god; he was considered either as adopted or as actually procreated by the god. This conception, in the first-mentioned form, of course, was not strange to Israel, either: the Psalmist makes God say to the king at his anointment on the Holy Mount: "Thou art my son; this day have I begotten thee." His anointment in the name of God made the incumbent of the throne responsible to God, not only as a viceroy is responsible to his sovereign but as a son is responsible to his father. Other peoples of the ancient East also knew this relationship of the king to the god; but in Babylonia it expressed itself merely by the fact that on the New Year holiday, as the day on which the world begins anew, the priest struck the king a symbolic blow on the cheek, which settled the matter for the rest of the year; in Egypt,

there were only intimate conversations between the
king and his divine father without any visible result.
Not so in Israel. Here, the prophet again and again
appeared before the king and actually called him to
account. This prophetic realism crystallized in the
divine message transmitted to David by the prophet
Nathan: God proposes to adopt David's son as His,
God's son, but if he sins, He will chastise him, as a
father chastises his son, and He will do it by the hand
of man, by the hand of the enemies of Israel, to
whom an Israel not upholding justice must succumb.

But the example of the attitude of the prophets to
the unfaithful kings is calculated still further to eluci-
date the nature of the relationship between Judaism
and civilization. The conflict appearing here is not
to be understood as one between civilization and
religion: it proceeded within a civilization (in the
widest sense of the term), namely between its guiding
principle, whose action had first produced it, and the
spheres of life, which more and more repudiated the
sovereignty of that principle. Often enough, therefore, the line of battle cut across religion itself,
namely, when established religious authority, person-
ified by the priesthood, sided with, and sanctioned,
power; in this case, religion, in order to maintain
itself, by virtue of its pact with power, in possession
of the particular sphere which the latter had assigned

to it, dissociated itself from the claim of the religious principle to be the mover of the whole. That coalition of established power and established authority was faced by the prophet as the man who had neither power nor authority. It is only in the early days of Israel, before the emergence of the situation which called forth the protest, that we find personalities such as Moses and Samuel, endowed at once with prophetic qualities and with history-making power and authority. Later, the powerlessness of the prophet was a typical feature of the age.

But the example chosen here can lead us yet deeper into the nature of our subject. For, the experience that the divine demand remains unfulfilled, engendered the Messianic promise, and just as the experience centered around the nonfulfilling king, the promise centers around the king who will bring the fulfillment. He is called Messiah, "the anointed," because he will at last carry out the mandate which the kings received upon their anointment. In him, man will at last go to meet God. Around him, at first Israel and then the city of Mankind will be built up as the fulfilled kingdom of God. But the latter is not conceived of as conquering and superseding a defective human civilization, but as hallowing, that is to say, purifying and perfecting it. When the life of man, with all its various spheres fully developed, becomes a united whole, hallowed to the divine, then, just as Abraham at the altar once called out the name of God over Canaan, the name of God will be called out over the whole earth as the domain over which He assumed government.

According to the Ancient-Persian doctrine, a world-smelting fire will transform the human substance: a new, divine work will replace the dilapidated work of man. Christianity, and also the apocalyptics of Hellenistic peripheral Judaism, developed this basic conception. Central Judaism rejected it. It took with it into its long exile the prophetic doctrine that in answer to man's return to God, the dislocated human substance will experience His redeeming force, which will complete the creation of man with man's co-operation. Civilization, despairing of itself, will offer itself up to God and be saved by Him.

This realistic faith in the future of God's image — in whose loss Judaism has never believed — cannot be dismissed with the cheap slogan "civilization optimism." It is the belief that just as every sinner can find forgiveness by "turning" to God, so can a sinful civilization. Just as man can hallow himself and gain admission to the holy without curtailing his existence, without "primitivizing" his way of life, thus human civilization, too, can without curtailment hallow itself and gain admission.

Here as everywhere else, Israel's religious-normative principle manifests itself as an essentially historical one. Just as its revelation, in distinction to the revelations of all other religions, presents itself as an incident of national history, so its highest goal, too, is historical in character. Here, the superhistorical molds the historical, but does not replace it.

With this historical faith — at once realistic and Messianic — inscribed both in its Book and in its soul, the Jewish people went forth into its worldwide exile and thus, in its majority, into a civilization whose religious-normative principle was the Christian. This situation was decisively determined by the fact that Christianity had its origin in a deformative late phase of Jewish Messianism, in which it strove, no longer to conquer history but to escape from it to purer spheres, while on the other hand, the group of peoples among which Christianity established itself had just started out to conquer history. Into their existence with its contradiction, the Jewish people was inserted with its existence and the contradiction thereof, enjoined to dwell among them, history-less, with its unfulfilled historical faith — among them who controlled history and whose faith commanded them to overcome history. We know what developed from this basic situation in the course of time.

The principle of our faith, the truth and justice of

God, which strives to fulfill itself in the domain of human life and human history, and which paints the Messianic picture of fulfillment on the firmament of that domain, continued to radiate from our Book, and some protagonists of the Christian faith were hit by its rays, so that one or the other of them conceived the idea that his people, like Israel of old, was enjoined to become a holy people and to hallow its civilization in all its departments. We ourselves were denied actualization of our principle in the world. In the era of dispersion, great things have happened within the Jewish community, in relation to God and to the brethren; but the development of a national personality expressing the divine intent was now made impossible to us by the fact that we were no longer a free and independent community. The Messianic idea, cut off from its natural area of realization, lost itself in late Gnostic speculation and storming collective ecstasy. And yet, in every hour of genuine self-rediscovery we knew: what matters is the test of history.

When at last we stepped out of the ghetto into the world, worse befell us from within than had ever befallen us from without: the foundation, the unique unity of people and religion, developed a deep rift, which has since become deeper and deeper. Even the event of our days, the re-entry of the Jews into the history of the nations by the rebuilding of a Jewish State, is most intimately affected and characterized by that rift. A home and the freedom to realize the principle of our being have been granted us anew, but Israel and the principle of its being have come apart. It is said that we are now assured of the renewal of a great Jewish civilization. But has a great civilization ever arisen otherwise than by the unfolding of such a basic principle? People try to conceal the rift by applying basic religious terms, such as God of Israel, and Messiah, to purely political processes; and the words, ready to hand, offer no resistance — but the reality which was once meant by them escapes any speech which does not mean just it, that is, the fulfillment of God's truth and justice on earth. True, it is a difficult, a tremendously difficult undertaking to drive the plowshare of the normative principle into the hard sod of political fact; but the right to lift a historical moment into the light of super-history can be bought no cheaper.

So much for the new Jewish community. But how about the Diaspora—still vigorously alive despite the immense destruction and devastation? Nowhere in it, as far as one can see, is there a powerful striving to heal the rift and to hallow our communal life. And if there, in our own country, the question of the existence of Judaism, that is, of the survival of the principle of Jewish being, may still be veiled by political controversy and danger, in the Diaspora, at this hour, it confronts us in its nakedness. Are we still truly Jews? Jews in our lives? Is Judaism still alive? And in Mankind, meanwhile, the great crisis of its civilizations and its civilization, which is a crisis of man, has broken out more and more manifestly. Every original tie seems to be dissevering, every original substance disintegrating. Man tastes nothingness and lets even it dissolve on his tongue; or he fills the space of an existence emptied of its meaning with the mass of his programs.

Where does the world stand? Is the ax laid to the roots of the trees — as a Jew on the Jordan once said, rightly and yet wrongly, that it was in his day—today, at another turn of the ages? And if it is, what is the condition of the roots themselves? Are they still healthy enough to send fresh sap into the remaining stump and to produce a fresh shoot from it? Can the roots be saved? How can they be saved? Who can save them? In whose charge are they?

Let us recognize ourselves: we, in whom, and in whom alone, that mysterious affirmation and negation

[25]

of civilization — affirmation and negation in one — was implanted at the origin of our existence, we are the keepers of the roots.

We are? How can we become it?

How can we become what we are?

THE SILENT QUESTION

SECOND ADDRESS

The Silent Question

FROM TIME TO TIME, I seem to hear a question echoing out of the depths of stillness. But he who asks it does not know that he is asking it and he to whom the question is addressed is not aware that he is being questioned. It is the question which the world of today, in utter unawareness, puts to religion. This is the question: "Art thou, perhaps, the power that can help me? Canst thou teach me to believe? Not in phantasmagoria and mystagogy, not in ideologies or in party programs, nor in cleverly thought-out and skillfully presented sophisms which appear true only while they are successful or have prospects of success, but in the Absolute and Irrefragable. Teach me to have faith in reality, in the verities of existence, so that life will afford some aim for me and existence will have some meaning. Who, indeed, can help me if thou canst not?"

We can take it for granted that the world of today will vehemently deny wishing to ask or even being capable of asking such a question. This world will passionately maintain that religion is an illusion — perhaps not even a beautiful one — and will support this contention with a clear conscience, for such is the assuredness of its conviction. In the innermost recesses of the heart, however, there where despair abides, the same question surges timidly upward again and again, only to be immediately repressed. But it will grow in strength; it will become strong.

The question is addressed to religion generally, to religion as such. But where is religion to be found? The question cannot be addressed to the isolated religious individual, for how can he measure up to such a claim at such a moment? It is only to the historic religions — or to some of them — that such a question can literally be addressed. But it is neither in their dogma nor in their ritual that the answer may lie; not in the one because its purpose is to formulate beliefs which are beyond conceptual thinking into conceptual propositions, not in the other because its object is to express the relation to the Unlimited by means of steadfast and regular performance. Both have their specific spheres of influence but neither is capable of helping the modern world to find faith. The only element in the historic religions which the world is justified in calling upon is that intrinsic reality of faith which is beyond all attempts at formulation and expression but exists in truth; it is *that* which constantly renews the fullness of its presence from the flow of personal life itself. This is the one thing that matters: the personal existence, which gives actuality to the essence of a religion and thus attests to its living force.

Whosoever listens closely to the question of which I speak, observes that it is also addressed to Judaism and, indeed, that Judaism is included in the foremost ranks of those religions to which the appeal is made. I have, recently, received communications from many parts of the world from which it can be sensed that clarification and leadership are expected of Judaism. It can be sensed, too, that many of these correspondents are speaking for the many more who remain silent. That the world expects something from Judaism is in itself a new phenomenon. For centuries, the deeper spiritual content of Judaism was either unknown or given scant attention, for the reason perhaps that, during the period of the ghetto, the underlying reality of Jewish life was hardly glimpsed by the outside world, while, during the emancipation period, Jews only — not Judaism — appeared upon the open scene.

A change seems to be taking place. Why? Is it

because of the massacre of millions of Jews? That does not explain it. Or is it because of the establishment of a Jewish State? That does not explain it either. And yet, both of these events are basically part of the reason why the real content of Judaism is beginning to become more perceptible. These astounding phenomena of dying and living have at last brought before the world the fact of the existence of Jewry as a fact of particular significance, and from this point Judaism itself begins to be seen. Now the world has gradually begun to perceive that within Judaism there is something which has its special contribution to make, in a special way, to the spiritual needs of the present time. It is only possible to realize this if Judaism is regarded in its entirety, in its whole way, from the Decalogue to Hasidism, in the course of which its peculiar tendencies have evolved in an increasingly comprehensive manner.

This "entireness," these fundamental tendencies and their evolution, are, for the most part, still unrecognized even by the Jews themselves, even by those who are earnestly seeking the pathway of truth. This becomes manifest when we consider those amongst our spiritually representative Jewish contemporaries whose religious needs have remained unsatisfied by Judaism. It is highly characteristic that, in the springtime of modern society, spiritually significant Jews turned to Christianity, not for the sake of Christian religion but for the sake of Christian culture, whereas today the sympathies worth noting that spiritual Jews feel for Christianity are rooted rather in a sense of religious lack and a feeling of religious longing.

Let us consider two examples which will make my meaning clear and which will plunge us deeper into our purpose of examining the religious significance of Judaism for the world of today. The one example is afforded by Bergson, the thinker who, like Nietzsche, built up his philosophy on the affirmation of life but, in contrast to Nietzsche, regarded not power, but participation in creation, as the essence of life. Consequently, again in contrast to Nietzsche, he did not fight against religion but extolled it as the peak of human life. The other example is to be found in Simone Weil, who died young, and the legacy of whose writings expresses a strong and theologically far-reaching negation of life, leading to the negation of the individual as well as of society as a whole. Both Bergson and Simone Weil were Jews. Both were convinced that in Christian mysticism they had found the religious truth they were seeking. Bergson still saw in the prophets of Israel the forerunners of Christianity, whereas Simone Weil simply cast aside both Israel and Judaism. Neither was converted to Christianity — Bergson probably because it went

against the grain to leave the community of the op-
pressed and persecuted, Simone Weil for reasons
arising from her concept of religion which, apparently,
led her to believe that the Church was still far too
Jewish.

Let us examine how Judaism appeared to each of
these and how the Judaism which they saw relates to
the actuality of the Jewish faith, to that "entireness"
which has developed in the course of time and of
which, as I have already pointed out, most Jews today
still remain ignorant.

The image of Judaism conceived by Bergson is
the conventional Christian one, the origin of which
lies in the endeavor to depict the new religion as a
release from the yoke of the older one. This picture
is of a God of justice Who exercised justice essentially
on His own people, Israel, being followed by a God
of love, of love for humanity as a whole. For Bergson,
therefore, Christianity represents a human conscience
rather than a social conscience, a dynamic code as
opposed to a static code, and the ethics of the open
soul as opposed to the ethics of the closed soul.

Simone Weil takes the same line but goes much
further. She reproaches Israel with idolatry, with the
only idolatry she considers a real one, the service of
the collectivity, which she, utilizing a simile of Plato,
calls "the Great Beast." Gregariousness is the realm

of Satan, for the collectivity arrogates to itself the right to dictate to the individual what is good and what is evil. It interposes itself between God and the soul; it even supplants God and sets itself up in God's place. In ancient Rome, Simone Weil sees the "Great Beast" as the atheistic materialist who worships only himself. Israel, however, is to her the "Great Beast" in religious disguise, and its God the God it deserved, a ponderous God, a God "of the flesh," a tribal God—ultimately, nothing but the deification of the nation. The Pharisees, whom Simone Weil obviously came to know only through the controversies of the New Testament, are defined by her as a group "who were virtuous only out of obedience to the Great Beast." Everything that was hateful to her in more recent history such as capitalism and Marxism, the intolerance of the Church, and modern nationalism, was ascribed by her to the influence of what she called the "totalitarianism" of Israel.

Bergson accepted the principle of social life as a transition stage; for Simone Weil, who, by the way, was, for a while, actively associated with the extreme Left, it was the great obstacle. For both, Israel was its embodiment, and both strove to surmount it through Christianity, in which Bergson found the purely human element, Simone Weil, on the other hand, the supernatural.

Seldom has it been so evident as in this instance how a half-truth can be more misleading than a total error. (As far as Simone Weil is concerned, it is, indeed, scarcely a quarter-truth.)

The real definition of the social principle of the religion of Israel is something considerably different from Bergson's conception and something entirely different from Simone Weil's.

It is true, the group which is welded together out of families and tribes under the influence of a common belief in God and becomes a people is understood in Israel as a religious category. But this is not the actual people, not that which the prophet who harangues the people sees assembled around him. The religious character of the people consists emphatically in that something different is intended for it from what it is now, that it is destined for something different — that it should become a true people, the "People of God." Precisely in the religion of Israel is it impossible to make an idol of the people as a whole, for the religious attitude to the community is inherently critical and postulative. Whoever ascribes to the nation or to the community the attributes of the absolute and of self-sufficiency betrays the religion of Israel.

What, however, does it mean to become a "people ow God?" A common belief in God and service to His name do not constitute a people of God. Becoming a

[36]

people of God means rather that the attributes of God revealed to it, justice and love, are to be made effective in its own life, in the lives of its members with one another: justice materialized in the indirect mutual relationships of these individuals; love in their direct mutual relationships rooted in their personal existence. Of the two, however, love is the higher, the transcending principle. This becomes unequivocally clear from the fact that man cannot be just to God; he can, however, and should, love God. And it is the love of God which transfers itself to man; "God loves the stranger," we are told, "so thou too shalt love him." The man who loves God loves also him whom God loves.

It is not true that the God of the Bible has, as Simone Weil expresses it, "never until the Exile spoken to the soul of man." He has always spoken to the soul of the individuals, even in the time of the Decalogue; to whom other, if not to the soul of the individual, can the injunction be given, not to covet, that is to say, not to be envious of what is another's? But God speaks to individuals according to their real existence, and this means, in the pre-exilic period, as members of the people into which they are incorporated and from which they are undetachable. The Ten Commandments are not addressed to the collective "You," but all of them to a single "Thou"; this

"Thou" means every individual, and as every individual is yet thoroughly embedded in the nation, he is thus addressed as a part of it. It is only in the degree to which the individual, in the course of historic reality, discovers himself and becomes aware of himself that God speaks to him as such. But even in the most highly individualized times that "Thou" still concerns every single individual so long as he does not intentionally shut himself away from it.

Bergson's conventional differentiation between Jewish particularism and Christian universalism is equally unfounded. According to Amos, the earliest of the "literary" prophets, who significantly takes as his example the arch enemies of Israel, the wanderings of all peoples are directed by God Himself. The prophet states that, not as something new but as something generally known. This is, indeed, a universalism not of the individuals but of the nations, through which it reaches out to the individuals. Within this universalism, however, there is a particularization of vocation: Israel shall begin the work of the materialization of God's justice and love on earth; Israel shall be "the first-fruits of His harvest."

It is not true that Israel has not accorded to spiritual inwardness its rightful place; rather, it has not contented itself with it. Its teachings contest the self-sufficiency of the soul: inward truth must become real life, otherwise it does not remain truth. A drop of Messianic consummation must be mingled with every hour; otherwise the hour is godless, despite all piety and devoutness.

Accordingly, what may be called the social principle of Israel's religion is fundamentally dissimilar from any "Great Beast." It is concerned with social humanity, for human society is here legitimate only if built upon real relationships between its members; and humanity is taken in its religious meaning, because real relationship to God cannot be achieved on earth if real relationships to the world and to mankind are lacking. Both love of the Creator and love of that which He has created are finally one and the same.

In order to achieve this unity, man must indeed accept creation from God's hands, not in order to possess it, but lovingly to take part in the still uncompleted work of creation. Creation is incomplete because discord still reigns within it, and peace can only emerge from the created. That is why, in Jewish tradition, he who brings about peace is called the companion of God in the work of creation. This concept of man's vocation as a co-worker with God is emphasized by Bergson as the goal of that mysticism which he glorifies and which he does not find in Judaism; it is, however, a fundamentally Jewish concept.

[39]

Both Bergson and Simone Weil turned away from a Judaism they did not know; in actual fact, they turned aside from a conventional conception of Judaism created by Christianity. But while Bergson was close to true Judaism which he did not know, Simone Weil was remote from it, too. When she referred to the God of Israel as a "natural" God and to that of Christianity as a "supernatural" God, she failed entirely to understand the character of the former inasmuch as He is not "natural" but is the God of nature as well as the God of spirit — and is superior to both nature and spirit alike. But even if Simone Weil had known the true God of Israel, she would not have been satisfied, for He turns toward nature, which He dominates, whereas Simone Weil sought flight from nature as well as from society: reality had become intolerable to her and, for her, God was the power which led her away from it. But that is definitely not the way of the God of Israel; such a way would be the very opposite of His relations toward His creation and His creatures. He has placed man in the center of reality in order that he should face up to it. Simone Weil's idea was to serve mankind and so she again and again took to heavy manual labor on the land, but her soul was always put to flight by reality. And she began with her own reality: she contested the "I"; it was one's duty, she thought, to slay the "I" in oneself. We possess nothing in this world," she wrote, "other than the power to say I. This is what we should yield up to God, and that is what we should destroy." Such a basic orientation is, indeed, diametrically opposed to Judaism; for the real relationship taught by Judaism is a bridge which spans across two firm pillars, man's "I" and the "I" of his eternal partner. It is thus the relation between man and God, thus also the relation between man and man. Judaism rejects the "I" that connotes selfishness and pride, but it welcomes and affirms the "I" of the real relationship, the "I" of the partnership between I and Thou, the "I" of love. For love does not invalidate the "I"; on the contrary, it binds the "I" more closely to the "Thou." It does not say: "Thou art loved" but "I love thee." The same applies to the "'We," about which Simone Weil said: "one should not be I and even less should one be We." Judaism rejects the "We" of group egotism, of national conceit and party exclusiveness, but it postulates that "We" which arises from the real relationships of its components and which maintains genuine relations with other groups, the "We" which may say in truth: "*Our* father."

Simone Weil knew neither the old religion of Israel nor its later way, in which the changed conditions of history brought about a new display of its

basic elements. Bergson knew the prophets of Israel,
yet without realizing how in their messages the principle of justice which he found in them was comple-
mented by the principle of love; but he knew not the
road taken by the Jewish religion and consequently
he did not consider the prophets in connection with
the whole of Jewish religious history. The prophets
protest against the religious failure of Israel, against
the fact that God's demand to create a place on earth
for His justice and His love has not been sufficiently
complied with — neither by the people nor by the
individuals within it — at least not in the measure
compatible with the strength available and under the
prevailing conditions. And the seed of the prophets is
springing up; though late, it is sprouting into stronger
and stronger growth. In the Diaspora, it is true, a
comprehensive realization of the principle of justice
could not be aspired to, since that would have required
an autonomous national entity, autonomous national
institutions, which could only be hoped for with the
return to the Holy Land; but the higher, the decisive principle which alone can knit together the
relationship to God and the relationship to man —
the principle of love — requires neither organiza-
tions nor institutions but can be given effect at
any time, at any place. The will to realization was
not, however, confined to the individual. Within the

communal form of life adopted in the place of a
state — that is, the local communities — active love
in the guise of mutual help recurs as a basic social
element. This structure found its perfection about
two centuries ago in Hasidism, which was built on
little communities bound together by brotherly love.
An inner religious development of the highest significance corresponds to that tendency, the striving to
bridge the gulf between love of God and love of man.
Again the Hasidic movement succeeded in giving full
effect to this striving. It teaches that the true meaning
of love of one's neighbor is not that it is a command
from God which we are to fulfill, but that through it
and in it we meet God. This is shown by the interpretation of this command. It is not just written:
"Love thy neighbor as thyself," as though the sentence
ended there, but it goes on: "Love thy neighbor as
thyself, I am the Lord." The grammatical construction
of the original text shows quite clearly that the meaning is: You shall deal lovingly with your "neighbor,"
that is, with everyone you meet along life's road, and
you shall deal with him as with one equal to yourself.
The second part, however, adds: "I am the Lord" —
and here the Hasidic interpretation comes in: "You
think I am far away from you, but in your love for
your neighbor you will find Me; not in his love for

you but in yours for him." He who loves brings God and the world together.

The Hasidic teaching is the consummation of Judaism. And this is its message to all: *You yourself must begin.* Existence will remain meaningless for you if you yourself do not penetrate into it with active love and if you do not in this way discover its meaning for yourself. Everything is waiting to be hallowed by you; it is waiting to be disclosed in its meaning and to be realized in it by you. For the sake of this your beginning, God created the world. He has drawn it out of himself so that you may bring it closer to Him. Meet the world with the fullness of your being and you shall meet Him. That He Himself accepts from your hands what you have to give to the world, is His mercy. If you wish to believe, love!

Bergson speaks of an "active mysticism." Where is this to be found, if not here? Nowhere else is man's essential doing so closely bound up with the mystery of being. And for this very reason the answer to the silent question asked by the modern world is found herein. Will the world perceive it? But will Jewry itself perceive that its very existence depends upon the revival of its religious existence? The Jewish State may assure the future of a nation of Jews, even one with a culture of its own; Judaism will live only if it brings to life again the primeval Jewish relationship to God, the world and mankind.

[44]

THE DIALOGUE
BETWEEN HEAVEN AND EARTH

THIRD ADDRESS

The Dialogue between Heaven and Earth

T HE MOST IMPORTANT of all that the biblical view of existence has opened up for all times is clearly recognized by a comparison of Israel's Holy Writ with those holy books of the nations that originated independently of it. None of those books is, like it, full of a dialogue between Heaven and earth. It tells us how again and again God addresses man and is addressed by him. God announces to man what plan He has for the world; as the earliest of the book prophets puts it (Amos 4,13), God lets him know" his soliloquy," He discloses to him His will and calls upon him to take part in its realization. But man is no blind tool, he was created as a free being, free also vis-à-vis God, free to surrender to Him or to refuse himself to Him. To God's sovereign address, man gives

[47]

his autonomous answer; if he remains silent, his silence, too, is an answer. Very often we hear God's voice alone, as in the prophetical books, for the most part, where only in isolated cases—in certain accounts of visions, or in the diary-like records of Jeremiah — the prophet's reply becomes articulate, and sometimes these records actually assume a dialogic form; but even in all those passages where God alone speaks we are made to feel that the person addressed by Him answers with his wordless soul, that is to say, that he stands in the dialogic situation. And again, very often we hear the voice of man alone, as generally in the Psalms, where only in isolated cases the worshipper indicates the divine reply; but here, too, the dialogic situation is apparent; it is apparent to us that man, lamenting, suppliant, thanksgiving, praise-singing man, experiences himself as heard and understood, accepted and confirmed, by Him to Whom he addresses himself. The basic doctrine which fills the Hebrew Bible is that our life is a dialogue between the above and the below.

But does this still apply to our present-day life? Believers and unbelievers deny it. A view common among believers is that though everything contained in Scripture is literally true, though God did certainly speak to the men chosen by Him, yet, since then, the holy spirit has been taken from us, heaven is silent to us, and only through the books of the written and oral tradition is God's will made known to us as to what we shall do or not do; certainly, even today, the worshipper stands immediately before his Creator, but how could he dare, like the Psalmist, to report to the world words of personal reply, of personal granting as spoken immediately to him? And as for the unbelievers, it goes without saying that the atheists need not be mentioned at all, but only the adherents of a more or less philosophic God-concept, with which they cannot reconcile the idea of God's addressing, and being addressed by, man; to them, the entire dialogics of Scripture is nothing but a mythical figment, instructive from the point of view of the history of the human mind, but inapplicable to our life.

As against either opinion, a faithful and unprepossessed reader of Scripture must endorse the view he has learnt from it: what happened once happens now and always, and the fact of its happening to us is a guarantee of its having happened. The Bible has, in the form of a glorified remembrance, given vivid, decisive expression to an ever-recurrent happening. In the infinite language of events and situations, eternally changing, but plain to the truly attentive, transcendence speaks to our hearts at the essential moments of personal life. And there is a language in which we can answer it; it is the language of our actions and attitudes, our reactions and our abstentions; the totality of these answers is what we may call our answering-for-ourselves in the most proper sense of the expression. This fundamental interpretation of our existence we owe to the Hebrew Bible; and whenever we truly read it, our self-understanding is renewed and deepened.

II

But in Scripture, not only the individual, the community too, is addressed from above, in such a manner as is found in no other of the holy books of mankind.

Here the people, as a people, confronts God and receives, as a people, His never ceasing instruction. It, too, like the individual, is called upon to participate in the realization of the divine will on earth. Just as the individual is to hallow himself in his personal life, the people is to hallow itself in its communal life; it is to become a "holy people." Like the individual, it is free as to its answer to the divine call, free to say yes or no to God by its doing and its not-doing. The people is not a sum of individuals addressed by God, it is something existent beyond that, something essential and irreplaceable, meant by God as such, claimed by Him as such, and answerable to Him as such. God leads it and requires it to follow his sole leadership. He has created not only man as an individual, men as individuals, but also the human peoples; and He uses them, like the former, for His purpose, for the completion of His world-creation. He takes care of them in their history; not only Israel but all peoples are, as the prophet proclaims, led by Him to freedom when enslaved by other peoples, and in freedom they shall serve Him, as peoples, each in its own way and according to its own character. Though He reprimands Israel with especial severity because, contrary to its mandate, it has not fulfilled divine justice in the life of the community, yet He reprimands the other peoples as well, because they, who are also His childern, do not act toward each other as brothers should. Some day, however, so the prophecy runs (Isa. 2), the representatives of all of them will crowd round Mount Moriah and there, as Israel once did, alone, at Mount Sinai, receive that divine instruction on the great peace between the peoples. "The noble ones of the peoples are gathered together," so the Psalmist says (Ps. 47,10), "as the people of the God of Abraham" — of Abraham, who is called "the father of a multitude of nations," a description meaning more than genealogy. Since world history is the advance of the peoples toward this goal, it is, essentially, holy history.

This is also why in Scripture the divine voice addresses man not as an isolated individual but always as an individual member of the people. Even before there is a people of Israel, its father-to-be, Abraham, is addressed as such: he is to become "a blessing" in his seed. And in the legislation, both in the Decalogue and in the injunctions supplementing it, God again and again addresses Himself to a "thou" which is certainly the "thou" of each individual in each generation of the people, but as conceived in his connection with the people, at whose communal life that legislation is aimed, so that everyone, when a commandment conveys to him the will of God with regard to his own life, conceives himself as the individual condensation of the people. This basic view unfolds itself up to the highest level of human existence: "Thou art my servant, the Israel in whom I will be glorified," says God (Isa.49) to His elect: the man who fulfills the mandate given to the people embodies the truth of the people's existence.

From here, modern life, both of peoples and of persons, is judged and its sentence passed. This life is split in two: what is thought reprehensible in the relations between persons is thought commendable in the relations between peoples. This is contrary to the prophetic demand: the prophet (Amos 1, 2) accuses a people of sinning against another people

because it "remembered not the brotherly covenant."
But that split naturally continues into the life of
modern man as an individual: his existence is divided
into a private and a public one, which are governed
by very different laws. What he disapproves, in his
fellow man and in himself, in the former sphere, he
approves, in his fellow man and in himself, in the
latter: lying degrades the private person, but it well
befits the political partisan, provided that it is prac-
tised skillfully and successfully. This duality of moral
values is intolerable from the point of view of biblical
faith: here, deceit is under all circumstances regarded
as disgraceful (also, e.g., in the case of the patriarchs,
as we see from the prophetical criticism of Jacob and
from some other indications), even if it is prompted
by a desire to promote the cause of justice; in fact, in
the latter case, it is the more pernicious, since it
poisons and disintegrates the good which it is sup-
posed to serve.

If the first biblical axiom is: "Man is addressed by
God in his life," the second is: "The life of man is
meant by God as a unit."

III

As we have seen, in the biblical conception of
existence God addresses the human person and the

human people with a view to what shall be, what shall be realized through this person, through this people. This means that man is placed in freedom and that every hour in which he, in his current situation, feels himself to be addressed is an hour of genuine decision. In the first instance, of course, he decides only upon his own behavior, but by doing so he participates, in a measure which he is neither able nor authorized to determine, in the decision upon what the next hour will be like, and through this upon what the future generally will be like.

It is from here that the great biblical phenomenon of prophecy must be understood. The essential task of the prophets of Israel was not to foretell an already determined future, but to confront man and people in Israel, at each given moment, with the alternative that corresponded to the situation. It was not announced what would happen under any circumstances, but what would happen if the hearers of the message realized God's will, and what would happen if they refused themselves to its realization. The divine voice chose the prophet, as it were, for its "mouth," in order to bring home to man again and again, in the most immediate fashion, his freedom and its consequences. Even when the prophet did not speak in alternative form, but announced unconditionally that after such and such a time the catastrophe would happen, this announcement — as we learn from the paradigmatic Book of Jonah — nevertheless contained a hidden alternative: the people is driven into despair, but in precisely this state kindles the spark of "turning": the people turns to God — and is saved. By an extreme threat to existence, man is stirred to the depths of his soul and brought to a radical decision for God, but this his decision is at the same time a fateful decision in the strictest sense.

Postbiblical thinkers have pondered how the freedom of the human will and the resultant indetermination of the future can be reconciled with divine foresight and predetermination. Outstanding among all that has been said in the effort to overcome this contradiction is the well-known saying of Akiba's ("All is surveyed, and the power is given"), whose meaning is that to God, Who sees them together, the times do not appear in succession but in progress-less eternity, while in the progression of times, in which man lives, freedom reigns, at any given time, in the concrete moment of decision; beyond that, human wisdom has not attained. In the Bible itself, there is no pondering; it does not deal with the essence of God but with his manifestation to mankind; the reality of which it treats is that of the human world, and in it, the immutable truth of decision applies.

For guilty man, this means the decision to turn from his wrong way to the way of God. Here we see most clearly what it means in the biblical view that our answering-for-ourselves is essentially our answering to a divine address. The two great examples are Cain and David. Both have murdered (for so the Bible understands also David's deed, since it makes God's messenger say to him that he "slew Uriah the Hittite with the sword,") and both are called to account by God. Cain attempts evasion: "Am I my brother's keeper?" He is the man who shuns the dialogue with God. Not so David. He answers: "I have sinned against the Lord." This is the true answer: whomsoever one becomes guilty against, in truth one becomes guilty against God. David is the man who acknowledges the relation between God and himself, from which his answerability arises, and realizes that he has betrayed it.

The Hebrew Bible is concerned with the terrible and merciful fact of the *immediacy* between God and ourselves. Even in the dark hour after he has become guilty against his brother, man is not abandoned to the forces of chaos. God Himself seeks him out, and even when He comes to call him to account, His coming is salvation.

IV

But there is, in the biblical view, a third, widest sphere of divine utterance. God speaks not only to the individual and to the community, within the limits and under the conditions of a particular biographical or historical situation. Everything, being and becoming, nature and history, is essentially a divine pronouncement, an infinite context of signs meant to be perceived and understood by perceiving and understanding creatures.

But here, a fundamental difference exists between nature and human history. Nature, as a whole and in all its elements, enunciates something that may be regarded as an indirect self-communication of God to all those ready to receive it. This is what the psalm means that makes Heaven and earth "declare," wordlessly, the glory of God. Not so human history — not only because mankind, being placed in freedom, co-operates incessantly in shaping its course, but quite especially because, in nature, it is God the creator who speaks, and his creative act is never interrupted; in history, on the other hand, it is the revealing God that speaks, and revelation is essentially not a continuous process, but breaks in again and again upon the course of events and irradiates it. Nature is full of God's utterance, if one but hears it, but what is said here is always that one, though all-inclusive, something, that which the psalm calls the glory of God; in history however, times of great utterance, when the mark of divine direction is recognizable in the conjunction of events, alternate with, as it were, mute times, when everything that occurs in the human world and pretends to historical significance appears to us as empty of God, with nowhere a beckoning of His finger, nowhere a sign that He is present and acts upon this our historical hour. In such times it is difficult for the individual, and the more for the people, to understand themselves as addressed by God; the experience of concrete answerability recedes more and more, because, in the seemingly God-forsaken space of history, man unlearns from taking the relationship between God and himself seriously in the dialogic sense.

In an hour when the exiles in Babylon perceived God's passage through world history, in the hour when Cyrus was about to release them and send them home, the anonymous prophet of the exile, who like none before him felt called upon to interpret the history of peoples, in one of his pamphlets (Isa. 48, 16) made God say to Israel: "Never from the beginning have I spoken in secrecy." God's utterance in history is unconcealed, for it is intended to be heard by the peoples. But Isaiah, to whose book the pronouncements of the anonymous prophet have been attached, not only speaks (8, 17) of a time when God "hideth His face from the house of Jacob," but he also knows (28, 21) that there are times when we are unable to recognize and acknowledge God's own deeds in history as His deeds, so uncanny and "barbarous" do they seem to us. And the same chapter of the prophet of the exile (45) in which God says (v. 11): "Ask me of the things to come," states (v. 14 ff.) that in the hour of the liberation of peoples the masses whom Egypt put to forced labor and Ethiopia sold as slaves will immediately, with the chains of serfdom still on their bodies, as it were, turn to God, throw themselves down, and pray: "Verily Thou art a God That hideth Himself, O God of Israel, Saviour!" During the long periods of enslavement it seemed to them as though there were nothing divine any more and the world were irretrievably abandoned to the forces of tyranny; only now do they recognize that there is a Saviour, and that He is *one* — the Lord of History. And now they know and profess: He is a God That hides himself, or more exactly: the God That hides Himself and reveals Himself.

The Bible knows of God's hiding His face, of times when the contact between Heaven and earth seems to be interrupted. God seems to withdraw Himself utterly from the earth and no longer to participate in its existence. The space of history is then full of noise, but, as it were, empty of the divine breath. For one who believes in the living God, who knows about Him, and is fated to spend his life in a time of His hiddenness, it is very difficult to live.

There is a Psalm, the 82nd, in which life in a time of God's hiddenness is described in a picture of startling cruelty. It is assumed that God has entrusted the government of mankind to a host of angels and commanded them to realize justice on earth and to protect the weak, the poor, and the helpless from the encroachments of the wrongdoers. But they "judge unjustly" and "lift up the face of the wicked." Now the Psalmist envisions how God draws the unfaithful angels before his seat, judges them, and passes sentence upon them: they are to become mortal. But the Psalmist awakes from his vision and looks about him: iniquity still reigns on earth with unlimited power. And he cries to God: "Arise, O God, judge the earth!"

This cry is to be understood as a late, but even more powerful, echo of that bold speech of the patriarch arguing with God: "The judge of all the earth, will he not do justice?!" It reinforces and augments that speech; its implication is: will he allow injustice to reign further? And so the cry transmitted to us by Scripture becomes our own cry, which bursts from our hearts and rises to our lips in a time of God's hiddenness. For this is what the biblical word does to us: it confronts us with the human address as one that is heard and may look forward to an answer.

In this our own time, one asks again and again: how is a Jewish life still possible after Oswiecim? I would like to frame this question more correctly: how is a life with God still possible in a time in which there is an Oswiecim? The estrangement has become too cruel, the hiddenness too deep. One can still "believe" in the God who allowed those things to happen, but can one still speak to Him? Can one still hear His word? Can one still, as an individual and as a people, enter at all into a dialogic relationship with Him? Can one still call to Him? Dare we recommend to the survivors of Oswiecim, the Job of the gas chambers: "Call to Him, for He is kind, for His mercy endurest forever"?

But how about Job himself? He not only laments, but he charges that the "cruel" (30, 21) God has "removed his right" from him (27, 2) and thus that the judge of all the earth acts against justice. And he receives an answer from God. But what God says to him does not answer the charge; it does not even touch upon it. The true answer that Job receives is God's appearance only, only this that distance turns into nearness, that "his eye sees Him," (42, 5) that he

[61]

knows Him again. Nothing is explained, nothing adjusted; wrong has not become right, nor cruelty kindness. Nothing has happened but that man again hears God's address.

The mystery has remained unsolved, but it has become his, it has become man's.

And we?

We — by that is meant all those who have not got over what happened and will not get over it. How is it with us? Do we stand overcome before the hidden face of God as the tragic hero of the Greeks before faceless fate? No, rather even now we contend, we too, with God, even with Him, the Lord of Being, Whom we once, we here, chose for our Lord. We do not put up with earthly being, we struggle for its redemption, and struggling we appeal to the help of our Lord, Who is again and still a hiding one. In such a state we await His voice, whether it come out of the storm or out of a stillness which follows it. Though His coming appearance resemble no earlier one, we shall recognize again our cruel and merciful Lord.